Nathanael Emmons

A sermon delivered at Salem in New Hampshire

January 4, 1797

Nathanael Emmons

A sermon delivered at Salem in New Hampshire
January 4, 1797

ISBN/EAN: 9783337264826

Printed in Europe, USA, Canada, Australia, Japan

Cover: Foto ©Lupo / pixelio.de

More available books at **www.hansebooks.com**

A

S E R M O N,

DELIVERED AT Salem, IN *NEW-HAMPSHIRE*,

JANUARY 4, 1797,

AT THE

O R D I N A T I O N

OF THE

REV. John Smith, A. B.

TO THE

WORK OF THE MINISTRY

IN THAT PLACE.

———

BY Nathaniel Emmons, A. M.
PASTOR OF THE CHURCH IN FRANKLIN,
MASSACHUSETTS.

———

PRINTED BY George Hough, AT *CONCORD*.

M. DCC. XCVII.

ORDINATION SERMON, &c.

EZEKIEL II. 8.

But thou, son of man, hear what I say unto thee: Be not thou rebellious like that rebellious house.

THE children of Israel were once holiness to the Lord, and the first fruits of his increase. They served the Lord all the days of Joshua, and all the days of the Elders that outlived Joshua. But ever after that memorable period, they began to lose the spirit of religion, and became more and more corrupt, until they were carried into captivity, as a just punishment for their deep declension. In this deplorable situation, they continued to harden themselves in sin, and to pine away in their iniquities, until every appearance of spiritual life was gone. Then God was pleased to send Ezekiel to prophesy over the valley of dry bones, in order to raise them from spiritual death to spiritual life. And to prepare him for his arduous task, he forewarned him of his danger, and charged him to guard against it. " Son of man, I send thee to the children of Israel. Be not afraid of them, though

briars

briars and thorns be with thee, and thou doft dwell among fcorpions; be not afraid of their words, nor be difmayed at their looks, though they be a rebellious houfe. And thou fhalt fpeak my words unto them, whether they will hear, or whether they will forbear; for they are *moft* rebellious. But *thou*, fon of man, *bear* what I fay unto thee: Be not *thou* rebellious like *that* rebellious houfe." This was the fame as to fay, *I know the degeneracy of the times. I know the corruption and obftinacy of the people. I know they will ftop their ears and harden their hearts againft divine truth. And I know, that for this purpofe, they will ufe every method, by words and looks, to corrupt your heart, poifon your fentiments, and deftroy your influence. But I warn you to beware of men; and never fuffer yourfelf to be corrupted by thofe, whom you are fent to reprove and reform.* This divine caution applies to all who are called to bear the meffages of God to men; and naturally leads us, on this occafion, to fhew,

I. That Minifters are expofed to be corrupted by the people: And,

II. That it is their indifpenfable duty to guard againft it.

I. Let us confider, that Minifters are expofed to be corrupted by the people.

Though this be a very humiliating truth to Minifters as well as people, yet let us attend to the

evidence

evidence of it, with ferioufnefs and impartiality. And here I would obferve,

1. That Minifters *have been* corrupted by the people. This was the unhappy cafe of Aaron. While Mofes was detained on the Mount, the people were uneafy, and came to Aaron, and de-fired him to make them an idol. Tho' he knew, that he had no right to comply with this unreafon-able requeft, yet he finally yielded to the importu-nity of the people, and made them a golden god. Accordingly, when Mofes returned and reproved him for his conduct, he made no other excufe than the preffing importunity of the people. " And Mofes faid unto Aaron, What did this people un-to thee, that thou haft brought fo great a fin upon them ?" This very queftion carries an implication, that Aaron was corrupted. " And Aaron faid, Let not the anger of my lord wax hot : thou know-eft the people, that they are fet on mifchief. For they faid unto me, Make us gods which fhall go before us ; for as for this Mofes, the man that brought us up out of Egypt, we wot not what is become of him." This was a bafe infinuation to the difhonour of Mofes, and an artful addrefs to the vanity of Aaron, which was exactly fuited to corrupt his heart, and draw him from the path of duty. The event anfwered the defire and expecta-tion of thofe who were fet on mifchief ; for Aaron

was

was corrupted, and became " rebellious like that
rebellious houfe." The fame thing happened to
the fons and fucceffors of Aaron; for we find that
they were always corrupt, when the people were
corrupt. There was a great degeneracy in the
time of the Judges, when every man did what was
right in his own eyes; and that day of declenfion
proved a day of temptation to the Priefts, who
were carried away by the ftream of corruption.—
When Afa came to the throne, we are told, that
" for a long feafon Ifrael had been without the true
God, and *without a teaching Prieft*." A great number of the Priefts were actually put down, in the
reign of Jofiah, becaufe they had fallen into the
degeneracy of the times. And at the reformation,
in Hezekiah's day, there was fuch a fcarcity of
*un*corrupted Priefts, that the Levites were called
in to affift them in the difcharge of their office.—
Indeed, it was fo common for the Priefts to be involved in the corruptions of the people, that God
generally reproved them both together. By Jeremiah he fays, " A wonderful and horrible thing is
committed in the land : The Prophets prophefy
falfely, and the Priefts bear rule by their means ;
and my people love to have it fo." By the fame
Prophet he fays again, that he would remove Jerufalem from before his face, " Becaufe of all the
evil of the children of Ifrael, and of the children
of Judah, which they have done to provoke me to
                                              anger,

anger, they, their kings, their princes, and their
Priests." By Ezekiel he says of Judea, " Her
Priests have violated my law, and have profaned
my holy things ; they have put no difference between the holy and profane, neither have shewed
difference between the unclean and the clean." By
Micah he says of the house of Israel, " The heads
thereof judge for reward, and the *Priests* thereof
teach for hire, and the Prophets thereof divine for
money." By Zepheniah he says of the oppressing
city, " She obeyed not the voice, she received not
correction : she trusted not in the Lord, she drew
not near her God : her princes within her are roar-
ing lions, her judges are ravening wolves : her
Prophets are light and treacherous persons ; her
Priests have polluted the sanctuary, they have done
violence to the law."

Now if the Priests were always corrupt *when* the
people were corrupt, then it is natural to conclude,
that they were, in some measure at least, corrupted
by the people. But we are not left to mere con-
jecture in this case ; for God himself complains of
the people for being always disposed to corrupt
their teachers. " I brought you up from the land
of Egypt, and led you forty years through the wil-
derness, to possess the land of the Amorite. And
I raised up of your sons for Prophets, and of your
young men for Nazarites. Is it not even thus,
O ye children of Israel ? saith the Lord. But ye
gave

gave the Nazarites wine to drink, and commanded the Prophets, faying, Prophefy not." They meant to corrupt the friends of virtue, and the Minifters of religion, on purpofe to deftroy the influence of their example, and the force of their inftructions and admonitions : And they very rarely failed of accomplifhing their malignant purpofe. The experience of ages, therefore, loudly proclaims, that Minifters are expofed to be drawn from their duty, and involved in moral corruption, by the undue influence of the people.

2. The bare example of the people, in a day of declenfion, has a natural tendency to corrupt Minifters. Moral corruption is contagious, and endangers all who are obliged to come within the fphere of its influence. When the people become cold and dull, and averfe from every thing of a religious nature, Minifters are apt to imbibe and manifeft the fame fpirit. When the people become light and vain in their converfation, Minifters are apt to countenance and imitate their levity. When the people grow rich and gay and luxurious, Minifters are apt to fall into the fame loofe and corrupt habits. When the people indulge themfelves in idlenefs, diffipation, and vain amufements, Minifters are apt to be allured into their company, and become patrons and partakers of their fins. And when the people become loofe in their fentiments, and will not endure found doctrine, Minifters

ters are apt to conceal or pervert the great truths of the gospel, and preach smooth things, to secure the applause and friendship of the enemies of truth. The day of degeneracy is a day of danger to Ministers. The prevailing spirit and practice of the times, naturally tend to cool their zeal, weaken their virtue, and injure both the matter and manner of their preaching.—But though they are exposed to be corrupted by the bare example of the people, yet,

3. They are in much greater danger of being corrupted, by the positive endeavours and exertions of the people to draw them into sin. A corrupt people feel themselves obliged to take this course, in order to resist the energy of plain and faithful preaching. They know the power of divine truth, the force of pious example, and the influence of godly Ministers: and they feel unable to stand before these united means of conviction. To prevent, therefore, the pains of a wounded conscience, they endeavour, by various methods, to bring Ministers over to their own side, and form them agreeably to their own taste. Some treat them with peculiar respect, and flatter their vanity, to make them more yielding and compliant. Some load them with kindness, and endeavour to draw them aside, by the powerful cords of interest. Some invite them to their houses, and into their company, and urge them to small and seemingly harmless

B compliances,

compliances, and fo take advantage of their weaknefs. And fome ufe more harfh and imperious
methods, and attempt to *frighten* them from their
virtue and integrity.

Such methods as thefe, we find the children of
Ifrael often employed, to corrupt thofe who were
fent to them as meſſengers of the Lord of Hofts.
Sometimes they attacked their virtue and innocence,
" by giving them wine to drink." Sometimes
" they faid to the feers, See not; and to the prophets,
Prophefy not unto us right things, fpeak unto us
fmooth things, prophefy deceits :   Get out of the
way, turn afide out of the path, caufe the Holy
One of Ifrael to ceafe from before us." Sometimes
they threatened their Prophets with the terror of
their tongues :   " Come, faid they, let us devife
devices againft Jeremiah, and let us fmite him with
the *tongue*, and let us not give heed to any of his
words." Sometimes they employed their *frowning
looks* as well as hard words, to deter their teachers
from their duty, and make them rebellious like
themfelves. And fometimes " they commanded
their prophets, faying, Prophefy not." This rough
method Amaziah ufed to filence the prophet Amos.
" Amaziah faid unto Amos, O thou feer, go, flee
thee away into the land of Judah, and there eat
bread, and prophefy there: But prophefy not again
any more in Beth el : for it is the king's chapel,
and it is the king's court." And the council at
Jerufalem

Jerufalem laid the fame imperious prohibition upon the Apoftles. After mature deliberation, "they
called them in, and *commanded* them not to fpeak
at all nor teach in the name of Jefus." Jews and
Gentiles are the fame by nature, and therefore our
Lord taught his Minifters to expect the fame treat-
ment from the Gentiles, which the Prophets had
received from the Jews. "Blefled are ye, when
men fhall revile you and perfecute you, and fay all
manner of evil againft you falfely for my fake: for
fo perfecuted they the Prophets which were before
you." The conduct of both Jews and Gentiles
towards the Minifters of religion, is a demonftra-
tion of the natural difpofition of mankind, to ufe
every method in their power to corrupt the hearts
and deftroy the influence of thofe who are fent to
inftruct and reclaim them.——We are all by this
time convinced, I prefume, that Minifters are expofed to be corrupted by the people.—But if they
are expofed to this danger, then,

II. It is their indifpenfable duty to guard againft
it. *Son of man, hear what I fay unto thee: Be not
thou rebellious like that rebellious houfe.*

It is the dictate of common fenfe, that every man
ought to avoid every danger, which he knows,
and which he is able to avoid. Minifters know the
danger of being corrupted; and they are all able
to guard againft it. This appears from the con-
　　　　　　　　　　　　　　　　　　　　duct

duct of many, who have gone before them, in delivering the meffages of God to men. The faithful Prophets and Priefts, as well as pious Apoftles,
felt their expofedoefs to the frowns and flatteries of
the world; but they nobly refifted every effort to
allure or to awe them from their duty. The Prophet Samuel, who was early called to deliver the
meffages of God to Ifrael, faithfully difcharged his
office, and maintained his innocence and integrity
to the laft. Though he lived in a day of declenfion, and the people were weary of the divine go-
vernment; yet he would never yield to their corrupt inclinations, any further than God allowed
him to gratify their wifhes: So that he was able,
juft before his death, to make the moft folemn ap-
peal to their confciences, that he had walked up-
rightly before them all the days of his life. Eli-
jah fingly and nobly refifted the frowns of the
people, the reproach of the Prophets, and the
wrath of the king. Jeremiah was furrounded by
enemies, who threatened to defame his character,
and to deftroy his life, unlefs he would forbear to
reprove them for their fins, and admonifh them of
their danger: But he bravely defpifed their threats,
and faithfully difcharged his duty. And the pri-
mitive Preachers of the gofpel difplayed no lefs
magnanimity and firmnefs, in the courfe of their
miniftry. When Peter and John were *commanded*
not

not to preach in the name of Jefus, by the moft dignified character in the Jewifh nation, they boldly replied, " Whether it be right in the fight of God to hearken unto you more than unto God, judge ye: For we cannot but fpeak the things which we have feen and heard." But Paul met with the moft oppofition; and accordingly manifefted the moft chriftian fortitude and fidelity in preaching the gofpel. " Do I," fays he to the Galatians, " Do I now perfuade men, or God? Or do I feek to pleafe men? For if I yet pleafed men, I fhould not be the fervant of Chrift." He affures the Theffalonians, that he had made it his maxim as a Minifter, to pleafe God rather than men. " But as we were allowed of God to be put in truft with the gofpel, even fo we fpeak, not as pleafing men, but God which trieth our hearts." The conduct of thefe faithful fervants of God, gives us clear and ftriking evidence, that Minifters are *able*, and therefore *ought*, to guard againft all the peculiar dangers of their office. And to imprefs this plain and practical duty the more deeply on our minds, I would obferve,

1. That God has exprefsly commanded Minifters, to guard againft the attempts of thofe who would corrupt their hearts, and draw them afide from the path of duty. His command to Ezekiel on this fubject, is extremely pointed and folemn:
" Son

" Son of man, I fend thee to the children of Ifrael.
Be not afraid of them, though briars and thorns
be with thee, and thou doft dwell among fcorpions : be not afraid of their words, nor be difmayed
at their looks, though they be a *rebellious* houfe.
And thou fhalt fpeak my words unto them, whether they will hear, or whether they will forbear ;
for they are *moſt rebellious.* But *thou,* fon of man,
hear what I fay unto thee: Be not *thou* rebellious
like that rebellious houfe."—Very fimilar to this,
is the command which Chriſt gave to his Apoftles,
and to all their fucceffors in the miniftry. " Behold, I fend you forth as fheep in the midft of
wolves : be ye therefore wife as ferpents, and harmlefs as doves. *Beware of men.*"—Thefe commands
from God the Father, and the Lord Jefus Chriſt,
bind all the Minifters of the gofpel to guard againſt
the peculiar dangers of their facred office, and to
repel every temptation to unfaithfulnefs. It is their
indifpenfable duty, therefore, to view mankind in
the light in which the great Searcher of hearts has
reprefented them, and to be as careful to avoid
their corrupting influence, as they would be to
avoid the jaws of a wolf, or the poifon of a fcor-
pion.

2. They will forfeit the divine prefence and
protection, if they fuffer themfelves to be corrupted ; and therefore it is their indifpenfable duty to
guard

guard againſt it. While they continue faithful to
God, and plainly deliver his meſſages to men, he
has gracjouſly promiſed to be with them, and to
preſerve them from the power of their enemies.——
Upon this condition, he promiſed to ſtrengthen
and ſupport his prophet Ezekiel. " Son of man,
go, get thee unto the houſe of Iſrael, and ſpeak
with *my words* unto them. Behold, I have made
thy face ſtrong againſt their faces, and thy forehead ſtrong againſt their foreheads. As an adamant,
harder than flint, have I made thy forehead : fear
them nor, neither be diſmayed at their looks, tho'
they be a rebellious houſe."— The ſame promiſe of
ſupport he gave to Jeremiah, on the ſame condition. " Be not afraid of their faces : for I am
with thee, to deliver thee, faith the Lord. Behold,
I have made thee this day a defenced city, and an
iron pillar, and brazen walls againſt the whole land,
againſt the kings of Judah, againſt the princes
thereof, againſt the *Prieſts* thereof, and againſt the
people of the land. And they ſhall fight againſt
thee; but they ſhall not prevail againſt thee : for
I am with thee, faith the Lord, to deliver thee."—
Chriſt alſo gracjouſly promiſes to be with his Miniſters, ſo long as they ſtrictly adhere to his precepts
and appointments. " Go ye therefore and teach
all nations, baptizing them in the name of the Father, and of the Son, and of the Holy Ghoſt ;
teaching them to obſerve all things whatſoever I
have

have commanded you. And lo, I am with you always."——Thefe gracious promifes are all *conditional*, and are fo explained by God himfelf. He fays to Jeremiah, " Thou, therefore, gird up thy loins, and arife, and fpeak unto them ALL that I command.thee: be not difmayed at their faces; left *I confound thee before them.*" And this awful threatening, God tells the corrupt Priefts in the days of Malachi, he had actually executed upon them. " Therefore have I alfo made you contemptible and bafe before all the people, according as ye have not kept *my ways*, but have been partial in the law."——Now, Minifters have *great* reafon to defire the divine prefence and protection; for if God be with them, who can be againft them ? And they have *as much* reafon to fear his departure and difpleafure; for if *God* be *againft* them, *who* can be *for* them ? This ferious and weighty confideration ought to make them extremely careful, to regard *God* more than *men*; and never incur *his* difpleafure, in order to gain the favour, or to avoid the frowns, of their fellow worms.

3. If Minifters fuffer themfelves to be corrupted by the people, it deftroys their ufefulnefs. If they imbibe the fpirit of the people, and feel as they feel; if they follow the example of the people, and conduct as they conduct; or if they condefcend to preach fmooth things to pleafe the people;

people; they will totally deſtroy their miniſterial
uſefulneſs: For, as ſoon as the people perceive,
that they regard *them* more than *God*, and will
proſtitute their conſciences to gratify their unreaſonable deſires, they will deſpiſe their perſons, and
neglect their preaching. Time-ſerving Miniſters
generally have but few hearers. All men, whether
good or bad, inwardly deſpiſe looſe and unprinci-
pled Miniſters, let their talents be what they may.
And the ſame degree of criminality, which would
be ſcarcely obſervable in other men, is ſufficient
to deſtroy the character and uſefulneſs of thoſe
who ſuſtain the ſacred office of the Miniſtry. No
men are ſo completely uſeleſs and contemptible,
as thoſe Miniſters who have loſt all appearance of
religion, and become viſibly conformed to the ſpirit and manners of the world. For, as our Saviour ſays, " They are the ſalt of the earth : but
if the ſalt have loſt his favor, wherewith ſhall it be
ſalted ? it is thenceforth good for nothing, but to
be caſt out, and to be trodden under foot of men."
Hence the dignity of their character, and the importance of their office, lay Miniſters of the goſpel
under ſolemn obligation to keep themſelves un-
ſpotted from the world, and to preach the preaching which God bids them, whether their people
will hear, or whether they will forbear.

I muſt obſerve once more,

C   4. If

4. If Ministers suffer themselves to be carried down the stream of corruption, they become not only *useless*, but *destructive* to the people. Corrupt Ministers are always corrupters. The whole tendency of their practice and preaching is, to corrupt and destroy the souls of their people. Tho' they have lost the power of doing good, yet they retain the power of doing evil. They can do more than other men, to pull down the kingdom of Christ, and build up the kingdom of satan. And as they are more capable, so they are more disposed, than other men, to stifle the spirit of Religion, oppose the doctrines of the gospel, and strengthen the hearts and hands of the wicked. This is the character which God gives of the corrupt teachers in Israel. He says, " Shemaiah taught rebellion against the Lord." He says, the prophets of Samaria and Jerusalem " made Israel to *err*, strengthened the hands of *evil doers*, and *caused profaneness to go forth into all the land.*"——When the people have formed their Ministers after their own hearts, and made them rebellious like themselves, their Ministers will then fit them fast for destruction. So God declares to Israel, by his faithful prophet Hosea: " There shall be like people, like Priest : and I will *punish* them for their ways." And our Lord says, " If the blind lead the blind, both shall fall into the ditch." Thus Ministers will destroy both their

own

own fouls and the fouls of their people, if they fuffer themfelves to be corrupted by them. And can
there be a more folemn and awful confideration
than this, to conftrain them to abftain from all
appearance of evil ; to guard againft all the dangers of their office ; and to difcharge all the important duties of it, with fidelity and zeal! This
is our indifpenfable and infinitely important duty.

Having illuftrated the danger and duty of
Minifters, I now proceed to make a few

REFLECTIONS,

which naturally grow out of the fubject.

1. IT is now a very dangerous day to Minifters, in this young and flourifhing Republic.——
The people have fallen into a great and general
declenfion. As they have increafed, fo they have
finned. They have loft their original piety and
virtue, and become extremely loofe both in practice and in principle. Every fpecies of moral corruption has fpread through every part of our nation, and feized all ranks and claffes of men. Ar-
minianifm, univerfalifm, and deifm, have more or
lefs infected all our towns and parifhes ; and led
multitudes to renounce thofe duties and doctrines
of religion, in which they were early educated by
their pious parents and faithful Minifters. This
day of declenfion among the people, is a day of
great

great danger to the Preachers of the gofpel. While
iniquity abounds, and the love of many waxes
cold, even the moft faithful Minifters of the gofpel
are in danger of falling into the degeneracy of the
times. This is very evident from what has been
faid; and ftill more evident from the conduct of
thofe who fuftain the facred character. Many Minifters have already begun to degenerate with a
degenerate people. Some have loft that fpirit of
devotion, that ftrictnefs of life, and that purity of
fentiment, which was once fo confpicuous in the
Preachers of the gofpel. And fome have begun to
yield to the corrupt humours and unreafonable de-
fires of the people, in points of ferious and weighty
importance. Some yield to the *vicious*; and neglect
to condemn and reprove their fafhionable vices.
Some yield to the *heterodox*; and neglect to condemn and expofe their corrupt fentiments. Some
yield to moral finners; and neglect to preach thofe
doctrines of the gofpel, which are fo difagreeable
to their carnal hearts. And fome condefcend even
to difpenfe with the laws of Chrift, and admit thofe
to enjoy the ordinances of the gofpel, who are vifibly deftitute of the fcriptural qualifications.——
Thefe are ftriking inftances of Minifters yielding
to the corruptions of the times, contrary to the
dictates of their minds. And fuch inftances as
thefe are very numerous, and to be found all over
the

the land. How many Minifters neither preach
nor practife according to their own fentiments,
through fear of offending, and through defire of
pleafing, the people? This conduct weakens the
hands of faithful Minifters, and ftrengthens the
hands of thofe who wifh to corrupt them. The
prefent profpect is, that thofe who are the light of
the world, will lofe their luftre; and thofe who
are the falt of the earth, will lofe their favor; and
there will be like people, like Prieft.——Trying
times for Minifters are probably coming. And let
us all, who think we ftand, take heed left we fall.

2. Minifters need, at this day, to be well
qualified for their office.——Though religion has
decayed, yet knowledge has increafed. There are
men of letters, or at leaft men of information, in
every religious fociety. The people in general are
much more capable now, than they were formerly,
of judging of the talents and qualifications of Minifters. And as they are more critical in difcerning,
fo they are more fevere in cenfuring, every minif-
terial defect or imperfection. The corruption of
the times appears in nothing more vifibly, than in
the united oppofition of the people to *facred* things,
and to *facred* perfons. They feem determined to
bring down Minifters, and make reprifals upon
them, for their having fo long poffeffed the public
efteem and confidence. Thofe, therefore, who enter

ter into the Miniftry at fuch a day as this, need to
be well qualified for their great and arduous work.
If they affume the facred office, without any confiftent fcheme of religious fentiments, or any con-
fiderable ftock of theological knowledge, they will
very probably injure the caufe which they ought to
defend and promote. For people have loft their
former implicit faith in the opinions of Minifters,
and pay no refpeͨ to their bare affertions. They
demand evidence for every thing which their teachers call upon them to believe and praͨife. And
this renders it neceffary for Minifters to be mighty
in the Scriptures, and expert in reafoning upon divine fubjeͨs. They ought to be able to meet de-
ifts, univerfalifts, and all gainfayers, upon their
own ground, and expofe the fallacy and weaknefs
of their boafted arguments. There is reafon to
believe, that the late rapid increafe of error and
infidelity in this land, is partly owing to the ignorance of Minifters, who have never formed any
clear and confiftent fcheme of Divinity in their
own minds. They have fuffered error and infidelity to take root in their own congregations, through
a fenfe of their own infufficiency to maintain and
defend the truth. And this has led infidels and
others, to reprefent the Clergy as a weak, ignorant,
fuperftitious fet of men. Hence it highly concerns
the Minifters of the gofpel, at this day, to wipe
off fuch afperfions from their order, by poffeffing

and

and difplaying that knowledge, which may put to
filence the ignorance of foolifh men: It is prefumption for any man, to undertake to preach the
gofpel, without being able to prove the infpiration
of the Scriptures, and to defend the important
doctrines which the Bible contains. This is what
people now juftly expect; and if they are difap-
pointed, it will injure both them and thofe who
profefs to be their religious inftructors.

But *prudence*, as well as knowledge, is a neceffary qualification for a Minifter. He needs this,
to enable him to exhibit divine truth in the moft
profitable manner, and to efcape thofe fnares which
the enemies of truth will always endeavour to lay
for him. Our Lord was a *prudent* Preacher. His
prudence, however, did not confift in taking the
fafeft methods to conceal difagreeable doctrines;
but in delivering difagreeable doctrines at a proper
time, and in proper expreffions. How often did
his enemies attempt to entangle him in his talk?
And how often did he confound and filence them?
There are many, at this day, who feel the fame
oppofition to the Minifters of the gofpel, that the
Jews felt towards Chrift; and therefore they need
to be wife and prudent, as he was, in order to
avoid the fame fnares and dangers, which he, by
his prudence, avoided. Accordingly he has exprefsly enjoined it upon them, " to be wife as ferpents, and harmlefs as doves."

But Minifters of the gofpel, at this day of declenfion, need large meafures of Grace, as well as
of knowledge and prudence. They need to be
crucified to the world, and the world to them, by
the crofs of Chrift. They ought to be willing to
take up their crofs daily, and endure the afflictions
of the gofpel. They ought to feek the honour
which cometh from God, and renounce that which
cometh from men. They ought to favor the things
which be of God, and not thofe which be of men.
They ought to love God, and Chrift, and the fouls
of men, fo much, as to be willing to be poor, and
defpifed, and abufed by men, in the faithful difcharge of their duty. They ought, in a word, to
be fo holy, and harmlefs, and pure, and heavenly
minded, as to be proof againft all the frowns and
flatteries of thofe who wifh to weaken their hands,
difcourage their hearts, and deftroy their influence.
If thofe who enter upon the Miniftry are poffeffed
of thefe fuperior qualifications, they may hope,
through the divine goodnefs, to war a good war-
fare, to keep the faith, and endure unto the end,
fo as to receive that crown of righteoufnefs which
is referved for thofe who are faithful unto death.
But if any prefume to run before they are fent,
and to preach before they are qualified, they have
reafon to expect that they fhall one day fall into
the corruption of the times, and become a reproach
to the facred order, and a ftumbling to thofe whom
they ought to have reproved and reclaimed.

3. It is the duty of all good men, at this day especially, to aid and affist the Minifters of the gofpel in the difcharge of their office. No men have greater difficulties to encounter, than Minif-ters, and therefore no men ftand in more need of affiftance, than they. They are pleading the caufe of all good men, againft the united oppofition of all bad men. Good men, therefore, ought to do all in their power to countenance and affift them. And in compaffion to Minifters, God has been pleafed to lay his fpecial commands upon all good men to help them. The duties which good men owe to Minifters, are plainly pointed out, and ftrongly enjoined, in the word of God. I will read a number of plain paffages to this purpofe. " The Prieft's lips fhould keep knowledge, and *they fhould feek the law at his mouth :* for he is the mef-fenger of the Lord of Hofts." " Obey them that have the rule over you, and fubmit yourfelves : for they watch for your fouls, as they that muft give account." " We befeech you, brethren, to know them that labour among you, and are over you in the Lord, and admonifh you ; and *efteem* them very highly in love for their work fake." " Remember them that have the rule over you ; who have fpoken unto you the word of God ; whofe faith follow, confidering the end of their converfation." " Brethren, pray for us." " Now I befeech you, brethren, for the Lord Jefus Chrift's

D   fake,

sake, and for the love of the Spirit, that ye strive
together with me in your prayers to God for me,
that I may be delivered from them that believe
not." " Finally, brethren, pray for us, that the
word of the Lord may have free course, and be
glorified ; and *that we may be delivered from unrea-
sonable and wicked men.*"— These precepts require
good men, in particular, to *bear* their Ministers, to
revere their Ministers, to *esteem* their Ministers, and
to *pray* for their Ministers. It is high time, for all
real christians, to awake from their stupor, and by
their prayers and exertions, to aid the Ministers of
the gospel in their difficult and important work.
If christian professors would unite with christian
Ministers, in the common cause of christianity, we
might reasonably hope that religion would gain
ground, and vice and infidelity would every where
fall before it.

But it is time to conclude the Discourse, with
such Addresses as are usual on such an occasion as
this. And, in the first place, I turn to him, who
is about to take the Pastoral care of this people.

Dear Sir,

YOU are entering upon a work of great diffi-
culty and danger. You will fare better than any
who have gone before you in the Ministry, if you
should not meet with any who wish and endeavour
to draw you from the path of duty. The people,

to

to whom you are going to minifter, we prefume are as well difpofed towards the gofpel, and to-wards the Preachers of it, as religious focieties in general. But the corruptions of the times have reached this as well as other places, You are, therefore, entering upon the work of the Miniftry at a very dangerous period. And though we hope you are really friendly to God and to his caufe, yet the feeds of rebellion are not entirely deftroyed in your own heart. There is fomething ftill with-in you, which expofes you to be moved from your ftedfaftnefs. Moral corruption fpreads its poifon very infenfibly, and often gains the poffeffion of the heart before the man is aware. You cannot, therefore, be too watchful againft its pernicious influence. To defeat the defigns of thofe, who may wifh to weaken your hands and heart in the caufe of God, you cannot take a more direct and effec-tual method, than to become " *an Enfample to the flock.*" It is the proper bufinefs of Minifters to *fet*, and not to *follow*, example. Inftead of fuffering yourfelf to be formed to the fpirit and manners of others, make it your conftant aim and endeavour to form others to the fpirit of the gofpel and the life of religion. If your people perceive this to be your fteady and governing principle of action, they will have but little *hope*, and of confequence but little *courage*, to make the attempt of corrupting either your heart, your life, or your preaching. If

you

you appear to regard God more than man, and the good of your people more than their cenfure or applaufe, they will feel a power in your preaching, and a force in your example, which they can neither gainfay nor refift ; efpecially if you difcover, at the fame time, a readinefs to pleafe, and even to oblige them, in all things which are confiftent with the duties of your office. Confcience is always on the fide of the faithful Minifter, and againft every re-bellious child of Adam : And it is this, which gives every Minifter, who fpeaks for God, and with his words, the afcendency over the moft hardened and obftinate finners. Only fear God, and make his word the ftandard of your preaching, and you need not fear to deliver the moft difagreeable truths to your people, whether they will hear, or whether they will forbear ; for they will feel that there is a man of God among them.

A good foldier efteems it an honour to be call-ed to the poft of danger. And if you are a good foldier of Jefus Chrift, you will efteem it an ho-nour to plead his caufe in a day of declenfion. It is a caufe which will certainly prevail fomewhere; and if you do your duty, you may humbly hope that it will prevail in this place. But, fhould you be fo unhappy as to find religion decaying among your own people, and among thofe around you ; let it not damp your fpirit, but awaken you to be
more

more fervent in your devotions, more indefatigable in your studies, more zealous in your preaching, and more holy and exemplary in your living. The united exertions of the enemies of religion, ought to rouse the united exertions of those who are set for the defence of the gospel, to put a check upon the growing spirit of error and irreligion : and we hope you will not be wanting, in your desires and endeavours, to awaken stupid sinners to a sense of their danger and duty.

There can be no neuters in the cause of Christ. He that is not *for* him, must be *against* him ; and he that gathereth not with him, must scatter abroad. You must be conformed either to Christ or to the world. You must either preach rebellion against God, or bear your public testimony against it, both in preaching and in practice. On this day, of your solemn consecration to the sacred office, you are solemnly called upon to choose whom you will serve, whether Christ or his enemies. Be entreated to make a wise choice, and never depart from it, because the consequences will be infinitely important. So our Lord hath taught you, in the most striking language : " Who then (says he) is a faithful and wise servant, whom his Lord hath made ruler over his household, to give them meat in due season ? Blessed is that servant whom his Lord, when he cometh, shall find so doing. Veri-
ly

ly I fay unto you, that he fhall make him ruler
over all his goods. But and if that fervant fhall
fay in his heart, My Lord delayeth his coming;
and fhall begin to fmite his fellow fervants, and to
eat and drink with the drunken; the Lord of that
fervant fhall come in a day when he looketh not
for him, and in an hour that he is not aware of,
and fhall cut him afunder, and appoint him his
portion with the hypocrites : there fhall be weep-
ing and gnafhing of teeth."

Son of man, *bear* what your Lord faith unto you,
and be not thou rebellious, like fuch a rebellious
fervant : but be thou faithful unto death, and the
Lord, the righteous Judge, fhall give you a crown
of life, which fhall never fade away.

The Church and Congregation in this place,
will now indulge me in a free and friendly Addrefs
to them, on this folemn occafion.   ·

Brethren and Friends,
BEHOLD the man, whom you have fo unan-
imoufly chofen to take the Paftoral care of your
fouls. Receive him as a meffenger of the Lord of
Hofts, and feek the law at his mouth. Efteem him
highly in love for his work fake. Confider him as
a Minifter as well as a man, and pay refpect to the
Minifter in the man. Ceafe not to pray for him,
and to join with him in building up the Redeem-

er's kingdom. In this, and in this alone, you may reasonably desire him to be one with you: And in this, and in this alone, will he be willing to join with you, if he is a faithful servant of God. Never desire him to regard you more than God; and never become his enemies because he tells you the truth. This will be diftreffing to him, and deſtructive to yourſelves. He cannot ſerve you any longer than he ſerves God. If you ſhould be ſo unwiſe as to deſire him to conform to your unreaſonable wiſhes, and ſo ſucceſsful as to bring him to a conformity, you will injure both him and yourſelves. It appears from what has been ſaid, however, that the people are extremely prone to corrupt their Miniſters: And this affords ground to fear, that this people, who have been ſo remarkably unanimous in the choice of him, who is now to be ſet over them in the Lord, may nevertheleſs become diſpoſed to weaken his hands and diſcourage his heart, in the ſervice of their ſouls. Should you endeavour to do this, and ſucceed in it, how dreadful will be your ſituation, when you come to ſee, at the laſt day, that you have grieved the heart and deſtroyed the influence of one, who deſired, and endeavoured to promote, your eternal good! —But, on the other hand, what can afford you greater joy, than to be preſented before the univerſe, as friends to God, and to them who were workers together with him in building up his kingdom?

kingdom ? —You and your Paſtor are both in danger.   He is in danger from you, and you are in
danger from him.   The connection which may be
this day formed between you, will be infinitely intereſting to you all.   We beſeech you, Brethren
and Friends, to take heed how you *bear* your Mi-
niſter, how you *feel* towards him, and how you
treat him.   He can do but very little without you.
He needs your love, your prayers, and your aſſiſt-
ance.   He is called, like young Samuel, to bear
the meſſages of God to you, in a day of great de-
clenſion.   And if it be his heart's deſire and prayer
to God, that you may be ſaved ;   let it be your
heart's deſire and prayer to God, that he may be
both faithful and ſucceſsful.   And if you receive
a prophet in the name of a prophet, you ſhall receive a prophet's reward.

A M E N.

THE *CHARGE*.

BY THE REV. *Gyles Merrill*, MINISTER OF *PLASTOW* AND PART OF *HAVERHILL*.

GIVING the folemn Charge at our Ordinations of Minifters, as it is a practice warranted by apoftolic example, fo it well accords with our natural fentiments and feelings on fuch an occafion, as it, at once, prefents to the candidate a fummary of the duties he is to perform, and of the reafons inducing to wifdom, zeal and fidelity in the performance.

This being the part of the public tranfactions of this day, affigned me by the ordaining Council; requefting the filent, candid and ferious attention of the whole, I turn to the perfon here prefenting himfelf before the Lord, and before his people, and by the divinely inftituted and expreffive rite of the impofition of hands, we, in the name, and by the authority of Jefus Chrift, do feparate and ordain you, Mr. *JOHN SMITH*, to the office and work of the Gofpel Miniftry : And as you are called of God, in the courfe of his providence, to the ftated exercife of the Miniftry in this place, we therefore commit unto you the Paftoral care and overfight of this Church and Congregation, in *Salem* ; at the

E   fame

fame-time declaring you to be invefted with all the powers and privileges of the Evangelical Miniftry, and under obligation the moft facred and indifpen-fable, to preach the Word—to adminifter the Or-dinances of the Gofpel—to rule the houfe of God—to pronounce his bleffing on his people—and to affift, on proper occafions, in ordaining others to the fame important work and office.

Take thou, then, upon thee, this Miniftry, and the overfight of this flock, with pure intentions, with a ready mind, and with inflexible purpofes, through grace, of fulfilling the duties of your fta-tion with diligence and fidelity.

In order to this, look well to yourfelf, to your heart and to your life, to the views of your mind, to the exercifes of your heart, to the general tenor and to the particular fleps of your walk. The good Minifter implies the good man, and perfonal religion forms a diftinguifhing trait in the charac-ter of a Paftor according to God's own heart.

It is our prefumption and our hope, that you have received an unction from the Holy One. Be folicitous, Sir, to drink deep into the fpirit of the gofpel, to feel and exprefs its energy and its graces, to exemplify all the virtues of that religion which you are to recommend to others, and to be your-felf a model of that amiable character and life, to
which

which it is the defign of chriftianity to form thofe
to whom you minifter.'

As a ftated part of your duty, you are to *preach
the Word.* And we give it you in charge to take
heed, both as to the *matter* and the *manner* of your
preaching. The Bible is to be your rule. The
facred Scriptures muft be the ftandard of your
faith, of your life, of your preaching, and of all
your adminiftrations ; thefe muft, therefore, be the
fubject of your daily, ferious, prayerful and im-
partial ftudy. In your examination of the Scriptures, you are to compare *fpiritual things with fpiritual,* and conceive of each part according to the
analogy of faith, and the fcope of the whole ; not
diftinguifhing things between which there is no difference, nor blending together things which are in
themfelves diftinct.

The Chriftian fyftem, you will underftand and
reprefent as a religion of divine original, fufficient-
ly authenticated to gain rational belief ; a device
of unfearchable wifdom and benevolence, intended
and adapted to inftruct the ignorant, to relieve the
guilty, to form mankind to knowledge, piety, fo-
cial virtue, ufefulnefs and happinefs ; a religion
which, in its ftructure, is moft admirably fitted to
difplay the riches of free grace, while it eftablifhes
the neceffity of godlinefs and found morality.

This

This religion is to be the *subject matter* of your preaching; and the doctrines, the precepts, the prohibitions, the inſtitutions, the promiſes, the threatnings, and the examples of it, particularly that of Chriſt, are to be clearly opened, diſcreetly applied, faithfully repreſented, and ſtrongly enforced; that, through the concurring grace of the Spirit of God, of which the Goſpel is a miniſtration, they may hopefully operate for the inſtruction, conviction and converſion of ſinners, as well as for the edification, comfort and improvement of the ſanctified. You are to avoid curious queſtions and ſtrifes of words, as tending to ſubvert and confound your hearers; and to preach Chriſt crucified; faith in him, and repentance towards God; that love which originates from faith, and which is the fulfilling of the law; together with that *holineſs without which no man ſhall ſee the Lord.* Theſe things teach and exhort.

In regard to the *manner* of your preaching, let it be in a mode correſponding with the nature of your ſubject; grave, ſerious, plain, ſolemn and animated, pertinent to the ſeveral ages, claſſes and caſes of thoſe whom you addreſs. In this way, *feed the flock, the ſheep* and *the lambs,* endeavouring *to approve yourſelf unto God, a workman that needeth not to be aſhamed, rightly dividing the word of truth, and giving to every one his* particular *portion of meat in due ſeaſon.* But,

But, Sir, you muſt know, that the deſk is not
the only theatre on which you are to exert your
miniſterial talents; nor is preaching there, your
only employment. Your whole turn of mind, your
temper and ſpirit, your general converſation, your
occaſional viſits and intercourſes with your people,
and the habitual courſe of your life and complec-
tion of your example, muſt be a lively comment
on your preaching, and a ſplendid exemplification
of chriſtian graces and miniſterial abilities.

You are now inveſted with authority to admi-
niſter the Ordinances of Baptiſm and the Lord's
Supper : This muſt be done with *impartiality*, to
the proper ſubjects, as ſtated in the goſpel, making
a judicious difference between *the holy and profane*.

You are not only to feed, but to rule the flock :
Let this part of your duty be performed, not *as
lording it over God's heritage*, but in a manner that
may combine meekneſs, moderation and faithful-
neſs, with dignity, wiſdom and impartiality.—
Strain not the cords of church-diſcipline till they
break, nor relax them to countenance ſcandal and
diſorder.

The gift that is in you, by laying on the hands
of the Preſbytery, is not to be neglected, as it re-
ſpects the ordination of others. You muſt act here
with great caution and diſcretion. *Lay hands ſud-
denly*

denly on no man, left you be partaker of other men's fins ; but the things which thou haft received, before many witneffes, the fame commit thou to faithful men, who fhall be able alfo to teach others.

Your candle muft not be put under a bufhel, but in a candleftick, *holding forth the word of life :* There you muft burn and fhine, till you *fpend and are fpent.* You muft cultivate a fpirit of fortitude, and *endure hardinefs as a good foldier of Jefus Chrift :* Undifmayed with difficulties, unallured by entice-ments, let your *patience have its perfect work, and be thou faithful unto death.*

Although your own flock claims your more particular and ftated miniftrations, yet to them they are not to be wholly confined. Let your talents and benevolence be exerted for the general good of the Churches ; to eftablifh or reftore truth and love ; to heal their divifions ; to ftrengthen the hands, encourage the hearts, and promote the re-putation and ufefulnefs of their Paftors, joining your efforts and prayers with theirs, that *peace may be within the walls, and profperity within the palaces of* our *Jerufalem.*

There is one thing more too important to be omitted in an addrefs of this nature — It is this, that *all your fufficiency is of God,* and that the efficacy of all your moft vigorous adminiftrations depends on

his

his blefling; be then, O man of God, a man of prayer. To the God of all grace let humble, ardent and frequent application be made for wifdom, light, ftrength, animation and fortitude, to aid you in your work, and for the energy of his Spirit to give impreffion and efficacy to your adminiftrations.

Thefe things we give you in charge, before God, Angels, and this whole affembly. Motives to keep it, unrebukable, are not wanting; motives both awful and alluring.——We affectionately exhort you, by your explicit profeffion of the chriftian religion which you are to preach; by the vows implied in your Ordination; by your accountablenefs to the tribunal of Heaven; by the doom of the flothful fervant; by the blocd of fouls that will be found in the fkirts, and required at the hands, of the unfaithful; by the pleafures of a good confcience; by the approbation of God; by the crown of glory that fadeth not away; by every thing that is interefting and important, in time or eternity, to yourfelf or to your flock — we entreat and adjure you to *take heed to yourfelf*, and to *the miniftry you have received in the Lord to fulfil it*: And may God Almighty blefs you—render you a rich and lafting blefling—and grant that, having *turned many to righteoufnefs, you may fhine as the brightnefs of the firmament, and as a ftar for ever and ever.*

AMEN.

RIGHT HAND of FELLOWSHIP.

BY THE REV. MR. Peabody, OF ATKINSON.

THE great Apoſtle of the Gentiles, when taking a comparative view of *faith, hope, and cha-rity,* evidently gives a preference to the latter.

Correſpondent to this idea, is the principal ſcope of revelation, by which true chriſtianity is clearly diſcovered to be a ſyſtem of genuine benevolence, calculated to promote the greateſt harmony in ſociety, and the beſt intereſt of the Redeemer's kingdom among men.

This divine love meliorates the heart, rectifies human paſſions, dilates the mind, increaſes humility, directs the affections to proper objects, and gives the finiſhing ſtrokes to a character, amiable in the ſight of God and man.

By this heavenly affection, cenſorious bigotry retires, and true virtue and goodneſs are cheerfully embraced wherever they are diſcovered.

A trait ſo ornamental in the characters of individuals, ſhines with diſtinguiſhed luſtre, when conſpicuous in *ſocieties* who are connected together for the promotion of mutual happineſs; and it deſerves an additional encomium, being particularly
enforced

enforced in thoſe *ſacred Oracles which were given by inſpiration of* GOD, *and are profitable for doctrine, for reproof, for correction, for inſtruction in righteouſneſs; that the man of* GOD *may be perfect, throughly furniſh-ed unto all good works.*

Love to the brethren, is the principal criterion, by which we are aſſured, that we are the true diſciples of Chriſt. It is eſſential in an Ambaſſador of the Saviour of men; it is eſſential in ſiſter Churches, to be exhibited upon all proper occaſions, eſpecially upon our Ordination ſolemnities.

This brotherly affection glowed in the character of the Apoſtles of our Lord. Upon their com-miſſioning and ſending forth others to be their fel-low labourers, they diſcovered their cordial appro-bation of them, and their reſolution in the cauſe of the goſpel, by giving them the *Right Hand of Fellowſhip.*

In imitation of this example, this ſignificant rite has been in general uſe among chriſtians, in ſucceſſive periods, to the day in which we live.

The preſent ſolemn and joyful occaſion preſents us with an opportunity to exhibit our affection and eſteem in goſpel order, to you, *dear Sir,* unto whom, by the direction of this venerable Council, I give my right hand.——You will receive it as a token of our cordial approbation of you, as a faith-

ful ſervant of the Great Head of the Church, and
one with us in the office of the goſpel miniſtry.

We welcome you, my brother, into the goſpel
vineyard, to take a part with us in ſowing, plant-
ing, and watering, with an humble reliance upon
God for an ample increaſe.   We publicly propoſe
an interchange of kind offices, that we may be fel-
low helpers to each other in the Lord.   We wiſh
you a happy and ſucceſsful miniſtry, with a united,
liberal, and virtuous people.   Rejoicing with you
in your preſent proſpects, we commend you to the
care and direction of Him, who holds the ſtars in
his right hand, walks in the midſt of his golden
candleſticks, and who has promiſed to accompany
his faithful miniſtering ſervants to the end of the
world.

May you have the exalted happineſs of promot-
ing union and harmony among this people; of being inſtrumental in the hand of God, in reclaim-
ing the erroneous, awakening the careleſs, and in
ſerving the beſt intereſt of this Church and people,
that you may " *ſave yourſelf, and thoſe who hear you.*"
May you cloſely follow the example of Chriſt, in
his imitable perfections, exhibiting much of his
ſpirit in your daily walk and converſation, that
you may be an example to your flock.   And you
will not fail to take God's word for the rule of
your faith and practice, to exhibit that diſpoſition
which

which characterizes the true follower of the Lamb of God, of that open, benevolent temper, which has ever appeared conſpicuous in your predeceſſor among this people, who is now in the evening of life.

A genuine principle, ſpontaneouſly producing the fruits of righteouſnefs, will give you favour in the fight of God and man, and a title, through the Redeemer, to a bleſſed future inheritance.

Go forth then under the cheering influences of the *Sun of Righteouſneſs,* under the protection *of the great Shepherd;* truſt in him, and he will be your ſhield, and *exceeding great reward.*

And now, my brethren and friends of this Chriſtian Church and Society, we ſincerely congratulate you upon the preſent joyful and intereſting occaſion; when God in his providence, by the infirmities of age, has cauſed your venerable Paſtor to retire from his public labours, cordially to join with you in a re-ſettlement; that you have been, with ſo much unanimity, directed to the choice of one, in whoſe fidelity we have reaſon to rely, to take the over-fight of this flock, and to direct you into thoſe paths of truth and ſafety, which lead through life, through the vale of death, and to immortal joys.

Receive him, my friends, as a rich preſent from your *aſcended Lord;* and treat him accordingly.— You are not to expect in him, perfection. You

have

have *this treasure in an earthen vessel*; he is subject
to like passions with yourselves.   Treat him, therefore, with candour, with affection, and in the ex-
ercise of that charity which *hopeth all things*.   And
when you approach the throne of grace, let him
have a place in your minds, that through your
prayers he may receive blessings from above.

As you would hope for the smiles of Heaven,
cultivate peace and friendship among yourselves.
Consult the general good, and ever be ready, in
smaller matters, to agree to differ.

Guard against incendiaries, especially such as
are veiling themselves with pretences of their being
of some particular party in religion.   They in general are the greatest banes in society.——Study
therefore those things which make for peace, and
the God of peace will be with you.

May the blessings of Heaven descend, and rest
upon you, and your Pastor; animating you to the
most laudable pursuits, that you may rapidly pro-
gress toward perfection here, and be prepared for
those regions of glory, where there is increasing,
ceaseless light and joy, and where, shaded by the
tree of life, flow rivers of perpetual pleasure.

www.ingramcontent.com/pod-product-compliance
Lightning Source LLC
Chambersburg PA
CBHW021438090426
42739CB00009B/1543